seen.

known. ✓

loved. ♡

seen.

known.

loved.

seen.
known.
loved.

5 Truths About
Your Love Language and God

GARY CHAPMAN
& R. YORK MOORE

NORTHFIELD PUBLISHING
CHICAGO

Scriptures taken from the Holy Bible, New International Version®, NIV®. Copyright © 1973, 1978, 1984, 2011 by Biblica, Inc.™ Used by permission of Zondervan. All rights reserved worldwide. www.zondervan.com The "NIV" and "New International Version" are trademarks registered in the United States Patent and Trademark Office by Biblica, Inc.™

Edited by Elizabeth Cody Newenhuyse
Interior design: Erik M. Peterson
Cover design: Faceout Studios
Cover background texture copyright © 2019 by GCapture / Shutterstock (164083430). All rights reserved.
Icon illustrations by Faceout Studio

ISBN: 978-0-8024-1990-3

We hope you enjoy this book from Northfield Publishing. Our goal is to provide high-quality, thought-provoking books and products that connect truth to your real needs and challenges. For more information on other books and products that will help you with all your important relationships, go to northfield publishing.com or write to:

Northfield Publishing
820 N. La Salle Boulevard
Chicago, IL 60610

1 3 5 7 9 10 8 6 4 2

Printed in the United States of America

Contents

Introduction

WHAT ARE YOU LOOKING FOR? Many of the people we encounter are looking for more out of life. They are looking for meaning—for a purpose for existence. They want to sense that their life has value. They want to be connected to others and work together to make the world a better place.

In short, they want *to love and to be loved*. Both of us have met hundreds of people who have shared their struggles in life with us. Most have a history of broken relationships. Beneath all of these struggles is the cry for love. Those who study the human psyche agree that one of our deepest emotional needs is the need to feel loved, to feel that someone values me as a person even when I don't meet all of their expectations.

It was this reality that led me (Gary) to write *The 5 Love Languages: The Secret to Love That Lasts*. The book has sold millions of copies in English and has been translated and published in over fifty languages around the world. As a student of anthropology, I am amazed that these five love languages seem to have universal application.

The five love languages are Words of Affirmation, Acts of Service, Receiving Gifts, Quality Time, and Physical Touch. Out of those five, each of us has a "primary" love language. One of them speaks more deeply to us than the other four. Thus, the key is learning to discover and speak each other's love language. When this happens, we thrive and our relationships thrive. For example, thousands of married couples have indicated that this simple concept literally saved their marriage. Single adults have enhanced their understanding of their relationship with their parents and have enriched their dating relationships. (If you have never taken the free love language profile and discovered your own love language, you may want to join the thirty million who have at www.5lovelanguages.com.)

We will dig into these ideas in more depth in this book. They can have a great impact on your life—connecting you with the love you're searching for. Read on.

THE STRUGGLE

Looked at the news lately? When we see the state of our world, we may ask: If emotional love is so important, why do millions around the world fight instead of love? Where does this start?

For one thing, we're all pretty self-involved. Psychologists call it being "egocentric." Which isn't the same as being "egotistical," exactly. It's the idea that my world revolves around me. There is a positive aspect to this natural tendency: it means I eat, sleep, exercise—I take care of me. However, this egocentric tendency often leads to selfishness, and I come to approach all of life with the attitude "What's in this for me?" This attitude affects all of our behavior. Two selfish people cannot have a healthy relationship.

Love is the opposite of selfishness. Love thinks, "How can I enhance the lives of those I encounter?" True love is not just a feeling—it is an attitude with appropriate behavior. However, true love stimulates the emotions. Thus, when you choose to speak my "love language," I feel loved by you.

In addition to this focus on self, many people also suffer the fallout caused by a world gone wrong, from gut-wrenching trauma and life experiences beyond our control and doing. Our makeup is a mix of our own "self-focused" bent and the conditioning from our experiences. Together, there really isn't a person among us that isn't in need of the deep, restorative power of love.

THE SEARCH

So where do we turn? Some gain a measure of success through "positive thinking." Believe it, and it will happen! Positive thinking challenges us to focus on the positive aspects of our world rather than the negative, to focus on our opportunities rather than our failures, to make lemonade out of lemons, to look for the light rather than cursing the darkness. Thousands of books have been written on the power of positive thinking.

Keeping a positive attitude can help us in many ways. However, most of us will need more than the challenge to "think positively" if we are going to live lives of love. It is difficult to think positively when the negative is in your face daily or you don't feel very good about yourself. Still, we search.

Many have turned to the realm of the spiritual in search of such love. We believe they are looking in the right direction. In my (Gary's) studies of anthropology, I have explored world religions, including those of nonliterate cultures. First, I am astounded that in all human cultures there is a belief in a "spiritual" world. It seems that fundamental to human nature is the sense that there is more to the world than what is seen by the eye.

While my studies in world religions have not made me

an expert on spiritual matters, I have deeply explored and experienced the life-changing power of the Christian faith. I am not talking about Christianity as a religious system. I'm talking about personally and genuinely responding to the God whose very nature is love. I have found that love to be overwhelmingly satisfying. It is as though God's love is poured out into our hearts and meets our deep longing to be loved. His love stimulates our love—because we are loved, we are now able to genuinely love others.

Why then are so many religious people rude, harsh, and condemning of others? Where is Christian love? While just over 70 percent of the US population identifies as Christian, many of them are merely cultural Christians.[1] They call themselves Christian because they grew up in a largely Christian culture. More importantly, many have not yet personally and deeply responded to the love of God. They are, in fact, still searching for love. As are so many of us, whatever our spiritual beliefs. And until our deep need for love is met, we are not likely to become lovers ourselves.

FEELING ALONE?

Let's talk about you.

You may know in a general way that you're loved—by family, friends, maybe even by God—but you may not *feel* it. If you are like many people, you feel alone a lot of the time. However, the reality is, you are NOT alone in feeling alone. Millions of people struggle with these feelings and these questions. Why is this? Our experienced reality is an indicator of something deep within us that is pulling us . . . pulling us to who we were meant to be and into a relationship of love that we were made for, a relationship with God. That is what this book is all about.

You may have heard somewhere about the five love languages. Maybe you have a friend who says their marriage was helped by using these languages with their spouse. But you can go even deeper with these.

How does this work? What can we learn about God through the five love languages? How can we connect with His love—so we actually feel it?

That is what we are exploring in this little book.

GROWING UP FAR FROM GOD

First, a personal word.

As someone who grew up far from God, I (York) never, not once, thought about my love languages or my own spiritual condition or needs. As I was growing up, we were often homeless. And when we weren't homeless, my parents would hang a sign on our home: "The Moores, the Atheists."

We would keep a bin on the side of the home for Bible burning too. We weren't just indifferent to God; we were hostile to Him and to everything related to Him.

It wasn't until my third year in college that I began to pay attention to my soul and yearn for something more. After I experienced God's love for myself, I committed to sharing that love with as many people as possible. For the last thirty years now, I have shared God's love with hundreds of thousands of people through books, radio, television, but most importantly in one-on-one conversations over coffee, lingering after a message, or in the backyard. Here are two things I have concluded through all these experiences with others: First, *every single person* I've ever met has been deeply shaped either by love or lack of love, and second, *every single person* I've ever met desires to experience love differently, according to their love language!

Our desire, then, is to help you discover the answer to the cry of your heart and to help you find a consistent path to feel God's love. As you experience God's love through your love language, we believe you can discover how to become a lover too! We can love because we *are* loved.

CHAPTER 1

"You Are Loved": The Words That Change Everything

LOVE LANGUAGE: WORDS OF AFFIRMATION

LOVE IS THE SINGLE GREATEST FORCE the world has ever known. It has led to the rise and fall of empires, led many to give their very lives for others, and inspired countless poems, songs, books, plays, movies, articles, cards . . . it's everywhere. Before the invention of the internet and long before the evolution of social media, people would literally send handwritten letters to newspapers all over America, seeking advice from one of the world's experts on love and relationships—Ann Landers. Ann Landers was the pen name of Esther Pauline "Eppie" Lederer, the famous national columnist who, for almost fifty years, wrote the syndicated column, "Ask Ann Landers."

She was not a psychologist or counselor. But her practical, commonsense, compassionate advice found a huge audience. And she understood love. She once said, "Love is friendship that has caught fire. It is quiet understanding, mutual confidence, sharing and forgiving. It is loyalty through good and bad times. It settles for less than perfection and makes allowances for human weaknesses.... If you have love in your life, it can make up for a great many things you lack. If you don't have it, no matter what else there is, it's not enough."[1]

> Why do we often resist believing that we are loved or even lovable?

I love you. When someone speaks or texts or scribbles or shouts those words to us, everything changes. These words give us a sense of worth and an anchor against the rolling waves of life. When we are at our worst, when life seems to fall apart or when we've been deeply wounded, these words from a friend, partner, parent, or sibling can make all the difference. These three little words change it all, so why do we often resist believing that we are loved or even lovable?

Millions of us have been told that we are loved, but we don't believe it, we can't receive it, and so we continue to work to *feel* loved.

SOCIAL MEDIA AND HUMAN YEARNING

While the "Ask Ann Landers" column is long gone, we still "write in" for help with love through social media. Social media has made the conversation about love much more complex and ever-present. In some ways, social media has made the human yearning for love much more acute for many because now we have 24/7 access to examples of people living lives we wish we had. We scroll through our feeds and we see, in vivid pixels, lives of love all around us. Pulsing humanity bursting with smiles, accessorized with food, immersed in beautiful places or just being a couple in a cozy restaurant. Having fun. Hanging with friends. Showing off the new baby. And we contemplate our lives and feel inadequate.

At the same time, many of us rely on social media and the jolt of pleasure we get when someone "likes" a post of ours—to feel like we're seen, like we matter. As we are finding out, however, the heavier our use of social media, the lonelier we are becoming. In other words, because we are settling for a cheap substitute for true love, we are finding ourselves *feeling* less love, like drinking sea water to quench our thirst; when we settle for counterfeit love, all it does is leave us gasping for more.

NOT ENOUGH WORDS IN THE WORLD

Some people really, really need to hear the *actual words*. For people whose primary love language is words of affirmation, unsolicited compliments or expressions of encouragement mean everything! Hearing the actual words "I love you" makes their day. Hearing the reasons *behind* that love sends our spirits skyward.

The problem: Words of affirmation are powerful, but for many of us, we just can't get enough. Comments and likes in our social media feeds make us crave for more and more words of affirmation. The more we get, the more we want. Reagan, for example, is a words of affirmation woman. By her early thirties, Reagan had become a stay-at-home mother of two beautiful children. While she was living a life of love with her family, she began to compare herself to her peers. She often wondered if she was a good mom, if her little ones were having a good childhood, if her home life was one to be envied or if she was falling short. Reagan began to fill her days in between caring for her young children obsessing over her Instagram feed. Always striving for the cutest pictures that showed she was a good mom, that she had a good life, and, most of all, that she was loved. Her posts provided her with the words of affirmation that gave her instant gratification, but they were never enough—she hungered for more. Though Reagan was frequently *told* she was loved, she was not settled in that love. She spent more and more time watching the words of affirmation tumble and roll across her Instagram posts, but she did not *feel* loved.

Reagan's struggle is common to us all. This struggle comes from the reality that we were created for God's love. Reagan, as a words of affirmation person, was created by God uniquely to experience love primarily through words. The catch is that there just aren't enough words in the world to help her *feel* that love in such a way to satisfy her soul. For those of us who experience love primarily through words, we desperately need to hear the words of God to us: "'Though the mountains be shaken and the hills be removed, yet my unfailing love for you will not be shaken nor my covenant of peace be removed,' says the LORD, who has compassion on you."[2]

THE POWER OF GOD'S WORDS

God loves you. He has compassion for you. He sees you and is working to make peace with you. The words of affirmation that God gives us are so much more powerful than the temporary and often shallow words we get online. They are a true anchor for our soul.

Reread this single verse, placing your name into it. For Reagan, it would read, "'Though the mountains be shaken and the hills be removed, yet my unfailing love for Reagan will not be shaken nor my covenant of peace be removed,' says the LORD, who has compassion on Reagan."

God's words are powerful because within His words there is a love we don't have to work for or strive to maintain. God loves you. He *says* it, and you can experience that love on a daily basis. Particularly if you are a words of affirmation kind of man or woman, you can *feel* loved. You can live into God's love by hearing God's words. Through your mobile device, you can read God's words to you and experience love and companionship in a way you may never have thought possible. Most people are not Bible readers, but studies have demonstrated the fact that regular Bible reading reduces stress, produces peace, and helps people live lives of love and appreciation. Why is that? Simply because there is a power in the words of God's affirmation to us in the Bible that we cannot substitute with words from other people.

Consider these words of affirmation from Jesus, who invites us to find our source of satisfaction in Him: "I am the bread of life. Whoever comes to me will never go hungry, and whoever believes in me will never be thirsty."[3] Nobody in our lives, not even our partner, parents, or spouse, could say something like this to us—it would sound like nonsense. Only Jesus can speak these words of affirmation to us in a way that makes sense and has an impact on our lives. Our deepest longings and hunger for love and companionship are found in a relationship with Jesus. God promises that we will never go hungry or thirsty if we come to Him. He invites us to come to Him because He loves us with an everlasting love.

GOD SEES YOU!

Here's the reality: You ARE seen, you are NOT invisible. God wants you to know that He sees you at your best and your worst and He chooses to love you regardless. So often, *feeling* loved is about being seen. For words of affirmation people, we try desperately to make ourselves seen so that we can get the reward of being told we are seen and liked. We dread feeling invisible and work hard to receive the words of affirmation that help us feel confident that we are seen and loved. This is what is so incredible, for better and worse, about

> We dread feeling invisible.

social media. We can make ourselves seen in a way that was never possible before. We make ourselves seen, like Reagan, by posting pictures of our lives, snapshots that tell the world we are here. However, have you ever posted something only to have almost nobody "like" your post? What's even worse, perhaps, is that the only "like" you get on a post comes from your mom or grandmother. At the root of our strong desire to be seen is the yearning to feel loved.

Again, God sees you. In fact, God has been watching you and watching out for you since the very beginning. There is a poem in the Bible where the writer experiences God's love through realizing how intimately God has been involved in his life during a very dark and difficult time. Here's a portion of that poem—consider it for yourself:

> You have searched me, LORD,
>   and you know me.
> You know when I sit and when I rise;
>   you perceive my thoughts from afar. . . .
>
> Where can I go from your Spirit?
>   Where can I flee from your presence?
> If I go up to the heavens, you are there;
>   if I make my bed in the depths, you are there.

If I rise on the wings of the dawn,
   if I settle on the far side of the sea,
even there your hand will guide me,
   your right hand will hold me fast. . . .

For you created my inmost being;
   you knit me together in my mother's womb.
I praise you because I am fearfully and wonder
     fully made;
   your works are wonderful,
   I know that full well.[4]

Now, you may be living a happy life, maybe even a life of love. You may be living a life where you are yearning for more. You may be in difficult times like the poet who expressed these words to God. Whatever your story, each of us was made for a deeper love, a love that can only be experienced in a "friendship that has caught fire," where we are known, we are seen, and we are accepted with all our imperfections and weaknesses. This kind of love can only be experienced in a relationship with God.

REFOCUS
Resting in what God says about you

"I love you"—three words that change everything. When these words are experienced through a relationship with God, they don't just change our mood or our day— they change us from the inside out! God wants you to experience His love, to *feel* loved. He wants you to base your sense of worth and belonging on it, not through wishing and waiting for temporary external affirmations from others, but through His words. His words don't change, they don't fail; they are always relevant and applicable to our lives. God's love is an invitation to us to find our deepest sense of identity and worth in the context of a relationship with Him.

The great thing about love languages is that they work both ways. No matter what our primary love language is, God is loving us in many ways, and we can respond to God in kind. We both give and receive love, and there are many ways this happens—but mostly it happens through our primary love language on both the giving and receiving ends. For those of us who are words of affirmation types, we can learn to respond to God in love—again, through words of affirmation to Him. We call this praise and adoration.

Try it out. Even if you've never "prayed," or if prayer is already an everyday part of your life, try telling God that you love Him. See how your day is different in the end if you spend time giving God words of affirmation. God speaks your love language. He tells you that He loves you in many ways, that you are valuable to Him, that you matter. What would it look like if you spoke back to Him through your love language as well?

In your times alone throughout the day, in a car, an elevator, or simply in your heart, try speaking words of affirmation, or praise, to God. You can say things like, "God, you are so awesome," "God, I love you," "God, you are always there for me," or "God, you are . . . " (fill in the blank). If prayer is not something you do very often, keep it very simple. God will hear! When we do this, we often find ourselves becoming better lovers, *feeling* love as we express love through the words of our lips. We don't praise God in order to tell Him something about Himself He doesn't already know. God knows how awesome He is already. We speak words of affirmation to Him to help us connect our hearts to what is true about Him and in doing so, we *feel* His love within us. One way you can begin to do this is with the poem above, Psalm 139. Try speaking this poem out loud back to God right now and see how that makes you feel. When we hear words of affirmation coming out of our own mouths back to God, it helps us truly receive God's words to us. And it will help us to feel more love and give more love.

CHAPTER 2

You Are Seen: You Matter and So Do Your Actions

LOVE LANGUAGE: ACTS OF SERVICE

A LITTLE GIRL LOOKED OUT HER BEDROOM window to the flower bed below. Instead of the beautiful begonias she so loved, she saw weeds beginning to crowd out the dollops of red and white flowers. She loved her family flower bed and was alarmed to see it so invaded by ugliness and decided to take matters into her own hands. She thought she would surprise her mom and dad by taking on the weeds herself and so, with bucket in hand, she knelt and began to pull the intruders up by the roots as her dad had taught her. She pulled and pulled, trying hard not to uproot the beautiful flowers nestled next to the spiky, fuzzy weeds. Yanking up weed after weed, she'd place them into her bucket, which quickly filled. She was determined, believing that she alone would conquer the weeds and return the bed to its stately beauty.

After a while, however, she began to survey her progress, only to realize she wasn't getting very far at all. What she did weed was just a small part of the much bigger problem. Where she did pull, she also disturbed the tender roots of the flowers she so desperately wanted to save. As she gazed at the overrun patch, she sighed in defeat, realizing that the job was just too big for her. Overwhelmed, she put the bucket away, went inside, and washed her hands.

So often in life, we are like this little girl—working to make a difference, to make our world beautiful, only to realize that the problems of life are far too deeply rooted and pervasive. Over time, we put our buckets away and wash our hands, abandoning our belief and passion that what we do makes any difference at all.

HAVE YOU EVER WONDERED . . .

Have you ever wondered if what you do makes any difference? Have you ever sighed in defeat or realized your bucket of weeds was already full to overflowing with the problems of life? We start out so passionate, wanting to make a difference but in the grind of life, we slow down and often give up. We wonder if our actions are making any difference at all, if anyone *sees* us. Over time, we begin to realize that the problems of life are much bigger and more complex than we originally thought.

God wants you to know, however, that He sees you. He sees your big heart, He sees your strong desire to pull the weeds of your life and the world, and He sees that you are weary. He already knows the job is far too big for us—the world was never ours to change by ourselves. He also wants you to know that your actions *do* matter and that *you* matter. You are NOT irrelevant. Our actions and the intentions of our hearts are indicators, proof that we are our Heavenly Father's children. Just like the little girl in the window who wanted to make her home beautiful, we look out at a world full of weeds and we know it isn't supposed to be this way. The little girl knew the difference between beauty and fuzzy, scratchy weeds; and, just like that, we know the difference between the world that is and the world that is supposed to be.

ONE LIFE THAT HAS MADE A DIFFERENCE

One of the great heroes of our time is a man with a funny buzz cut and thick glasses who started a non-governmental organization to fight slavery. Gary Haugen was a lawyer for the US Department of Justice, but in 1997, he left his career to start the International Justice Mission, or IJM. IJM now operates globally and, by the time of the writing of this book, has rescued nearly 50,000 slaves! What's more, IJM has played an essential role in changing laws and providing training to law enforcement agencies all over the world. They have helped shape the human rights policies of foreign national governments, developed world-class research on trafficking, and have prosecuted countless perpetrators. Through the work of IJM, entire communities that used to be controlled by human trafficking rings are now flourishing slave-free! There are flower beds of people, entire communities actually, that used to be so choked by the weeds of injustice that one could hardly see hope for the future. Because of Gary Haugen and the IJM team, the red and white dollops of hope in these places of suffering are now flourishing with justice and beauty.

But what if Gary Haugen had not acted? What might the life of Jyoti look like today? Jyoti is one of the 50,000 slaves Gary's team has helped liberate from brothels and other forms of slavery. She was rescued when she was just six years of age. She, and many other children who have been liberated from sex trafficking because of IJM, is flourishing. Gary's decision to leave a successful career with the US

Department of Justice made a world of difference in Jyoti's life and community. There is a famous quote that says, "The only thing necessary for the triumph of evil is that good men do nothing." No one is quite sure who said it first, but it is a powerful truth.

The question is, how do we continue to fight for justice, hope for a better world, work for righteousness and beauty when we are just so tired? How did Gary and the team do it? Aren't they tired too? Isn't their bucket overflowing with weeds like ours? The real problems of our lives and world are complex and deep-rooted, and working to establish righteousness and beauty often leads us to unintentionally uproot what is good. So how did Gary and the team make such a difference?

ACTIONS FUELED BY LOVE

This is where love comes in. You see, our actions *do* matter, they *do* make a difference, but our actions are most powerful when they are fueled by love. Love has multiplicative, exponential power. Love transforms our simple desire to "do good" into something real and lasting.

> Our actions are most powerful when they are fueled by love.

How? God alone has the power to change our lives and our world, and through a relationship of love with Him, our buckets don't overflow with weeds and we don't grow weary of seeking after beauty and righteousness when we do it together with Him. This is exactly what Gary Haugen found when he began the International Justice Mission. He and the team realized early on that they needed the supernatural, exponential power of God's love to see them through! Gary and the IJM team start each day, all over the world, expressing their love to God through concerted times in prayer. They stop each day, all over the world, in the middle of the day to pray prayers of love and adoration to God. Through their commitment of love not only for those who are marginalized and oppressed, but also love to God, they have the fuel to carry on in a world of weeds and weariness.[1]

Again, love makes all the difference in the world. It isn't just something personal. In the Bible, there is a book of famous quotes called Proverbs. One of these famous quotes says, "Whoever pursues righteousness and love finds life, prosperity and honor."[2] The magic combination is righteousness *and* love. When these two come together, it is like nothing under the sun! Without love, our actions have no sustaining power, and we often grow weary, angry, and bitter. In the original language of this quote, the word for "prosperity" literally means "flourishing." So, a person who combines their strong inner desire for making things right and just with love finds life, flourishing, and honor. When these two meet, we have the sustaining power that overcomes a world of weeds and hopelessness. (See the connection between "flourishing" and "flowers"?)

What about "honor"? Pursuing righteousness and love together leads to honor, the *recognition* of accomplishment. When we live lives of love in the pursuit of making the world right, we are seen *and* known. What if, instead of going it alone, the little girl and her father made an afternoon of pulling the weeds together, taking time to laugh and encourage one another instead? Do you think this would have made much difference when the little girl's bucket filled or when she felt overwhelmed? At the end of the day, I'm sure her dad would have said, "Great job!," "We did it!," or "Way to go!" These are words of honor. People who are driven for justice often need to know that they are not irrelevant. They need the affirmation of being honored—there is nothing wrong with that.

TO MAKE THINGS RIGHT

The Bible teaches us that living a life of love and working toward a world made right *will* result in honor. We *will* be seen when we live lives of love and righteousness. The people who are most driven toward justice, however, often don't think a lot about love, and people who are all about love aren't usually the people who are marching in our streets or fighting systemic injustices. When the two come together, it is explosive! Remember, God has created us for love and that we experience love, actually *feel* loved, when we are loved through our primary love language. Our love language allows us to *feel* love, to experience love at the core of our being. People who receive love through the love language of acts of service are very often those of us who are passionate about justice. These people are normally action-oriented women and men who will not settle for the status quo of suffering, marginalization, and oppression. Like Gary and the little girl, they push toward a world made right and beautiful! They work toward a world they know *should* exist but *doesn't*. Simply put, acts of service people work to make things right.

ACTS OF SERVICE—AND YOU

Are you an acts of service kind of person? Remember, you can discover your love language for free at www.5love languages.com. If you are primarily driven by this love language, you will often find yourself expressing your care and concern for others and the world around you through actions. Conversely, you also experience love through the actions of others in your life. You interpret people's care for you through their actions. In your mind, talk is cheap, and people need to put their money where their mouths are, roll up their sleeves, and actually *do* something. You *feel* love from others when they see you, acknowledge you, and reciprocate through acts of care and concern.

Acts of service people are often big-picture people too. They are often willing to put their energy into serving the needs of others politically, socially, and relationally. They want to make the entire garden weed-free. That's why things like laziness, broken commitments, and inaction are so frustrating to these kinds of people. This is one of the ways we see how we are created by a big-picture God. The God of creation put things together with the big picture in mind. Beautiful streams flow into rivers, and rivers into lakes and oceans, which feed colonies of every beautiful species of mammal, fowl, insect, and sea creature. The God of creation did not just create individual, random-roaming beasts. There is balance and beauty in God's creation, and deep down, in the core of who we are, we know that and we seek that world of balance and beauty.

YOU ARE NOT IRRELEVANT!

The sad reality is that our world is broken. There *are* weeds. Children are sold into brothels. People are not kind and don't work for the good of the planet or for people. More than most, this bothers acts of service folks. For all our work, we often feel irrelevant, like the little girl with so much left undone and a bucket full of weeds. Over time, we find ourselves giving up on our best ideals, putting down the bucket, and washing our hands. Through a relationship with God, however, we can live into and experience love *through* the very work we do! We can *feel* loved through the camaraderie and recognition we experience from God, alongside others who are also in a relationship with Him.

> When we combine love with righteousness, we will flourish!

We can discover that we are not irrelevant and that the work can have meaning. When acts of service people try to go it alone, our buckets fill, the task seems hopeless, and we grow weary and bitter. On the other hand, when we combine love with righteousness, as Proverbs tells us, we will flourish!

God wants you to know that you *do* matter, that your life does have relevance. He wants you to know that your actions *can* make a difference if they are rooted in love. You see, we have been created to make a difference, to shape the world in a relationship with God. God didn't create us to sit under a tree and just take it all in. God did not create spectators; He created sons and daughters to work alongside Him in love, making a world of beauty, a world where we are striving to make things right.

REFOCUS:
Believing you matter

When we talk about God, it is important to realize that we are not talking about some idea of our own making. We are talking about the God who created roaring seas of wonder, covered the mountaintops with swirling snow, and filled the world with beautiful children bursting with hope and joy. God is real. He has made Himself known to us through three specific ways—first, through the world He has created. The God who made it all and is intimately engaged in every aspect of His creation is also intimately engaged with you. God sees you—you are *not* invisible to Him!

The second way God has made Himself known to us is through the Bible, where we see the great story of God, from creation to the end of time. In that Story, we see and we learn that God has a plan for the world and for us. God is in the process of making everything new again, of restoring what has been lost. God will rid the garden of weeds and make all things right and beautiful again. God's word to us in the Bible is how we know His love and how we can experience His greatest revelation to us—His Son, Jesus. Jesus came into the world to reveal God's love to us and to provide the means through which we can live into that love. Jesus is the very embodiment of our love language, for in Him and through Him we can experience a depth of love not possible through any other means.

Consider the words of Jesus and how they speak the love language of acts of service: "Consider how the wild flowers grow. They do not labor or spin. Yet I tell you, not even Solomon in all his splendor was dressed like one of these. If that is how God clothes the grass of the field, which is here today, and tomorrow is thrown into the fire, how much more will he clothe you—you of little faith!"[3]

Solomon was a fabulously wealthy king of ancient times. Jesus was addressing many people who did not feel very important and who did not have very much. He was giving them hope.

Even without your "labor or spinning" (like a spinning wheel making clothes), you have value to God. You are seen, known, and cared for. Whatever your work is, you may think it doesn't mean much in the world. You may think you only have significance if you're accomplishing something, if you're out there with that big bucket, pulling weeds and doing important things. But Jesus' words here demonstrate God's deep love and care for you. He "dresses" us in beauty like a field of wildflowers. Have you ever been physically "dressed in beauty"? Perhaps it was for a special occasion like a graduation or wedding, a day of honor or celebration. Perhaps it was a day for pictures or partying. Getting dressed in beauty is festive and special. As we live into a relationship of love with God, He sees us and celebrates us with honor as He clothes us with a beauty that is greater than a field of weed-free wildflowers.

God wants you to feel seen by experiencing His love. He wants you to find your greatest sense of purpose and accomplishment not through working hard but by living a life of love. God has a bigger picture in mind than just righting wrongs. He is at work to clothe us—and the rest of the world—in beauty. This bigger picture can come true in your life and through your actions when love and righteousness come together.

Now, some of you may be able to point to a clear moment in your life when you experienced God's love. You have made a decision to believe that God has clothed you in righteousness. Perhaps you would already consider yourself a follower of Jesus, a believer in God, a person who has been clothed in beauty, but you don't feel beautiful these days. Perhaps there is a cloud hanging over you, a darkness that prevents you from living into the joy and purpose of God's love. There are many reasons why this happens to us over time. Often, little by little, we walk away from God's love and toward the more immediate things that get us through the day. Sometimes these things are relationships that tear us down, the quick fix of physical pleasures, addictions, habits, or simply giving up on life altogether. We all have times in our lives when it is easier to take the path of pleasure rather than the hard work of love.

For many people who have already decided to live in God's love, we find ourselves from time to time needing a fresh start. Some people call this a moment of "rededication," a moment of decision when we recognize that we've walked away from love and admit our need to re-experience God's presence and power in our lives. If that is you, consider simply saying these words out loud to God right now:

"God, I want to live in Your love. Forgive me for the ways I've walked away from a life of love. Please come back to the center of my life. Fill me with Your joy and set me free from the things that are preventing me from knowing You."

CHAPTER 3

You Have Worth: The Gift of Being Accepted

LOVE LANGUAGE: RECEIVING GIFTS

CHRISTINE WORKED ALL DAY PREPPING special finger foods, selecting songs for the playlist, and decorating her apartment for yet another party. This wasn't just another fun social occasion. Christine's parties were always appreciated by her friends, who counted themselves lucky to have been invited. Christine took throwing parties to another level with her fabulous attention to detail and anticipation of guest needs. Most of all, Christine labored mentally each and every time with her commitment to giving a simple, inexpensive "party favor" for her guests. As if the parties she threw were not enough, Christine was famous for always sending her guests away at the end with something extra—a small framed photo from the night, a seasonal etched drinking glass, pocket warmers for the cold ride home. Her party favors were always thoughtful, sincere, and demonstrated something important about herself—this was how Christine showed love to people she cared about.

Underneath all the fun, however, Christine never got out of the parties what she put in. Her gifts were always well received, and she was thanked with words of affirmation, hugs, and promises of quality time around a cup of coffee, but she rarely *felt* loved in return. She longed to feel loved in the way she was trying to love those in her life.

This cycle of giving and not feeling loved in return came to a breaking point during one particular Christmas party where Christine had gone all out. Everything was set, flawless by even professional party planner standards. Guests began to arrive in fun and festive attire, bubbling with holiday cheer. Christine's famous party gifts were given on the way *in* this time, instead of on the way out! The food was perfect, the music was perfect, the gifts were perfect. Eventually, however, Christine found herself sitting in the hallway outside her apartment door, listening to the laughter of her guests at her own party. She wondered if they even realized she was gone. Christine felt like an unwanted guest in her own home, but why? She did not feel connected to those inside; she did not *feel* loved in return. In her hallway, all alone, a wave of anger, fear, bitterness, and despair swept over her and within her. "Why don't I get gifts like I give?" "Are people just using me?" "Don't they appreciate what I've given them?" "Am I missing something?"

WHAT GIFTS DO—AND DON'T DO—FOR US

Christine's struggles are not uncommon. She is a "gift giver," a person who experiences love through giving and receiving gifts. This third love language is spoken by those of us who thrive on the thoughtfulness and care behind gifts. We sense our value, our worth, based on the attentiveness gifts demonstrate to us. Gift givers long to feel worth through giving and receiving gifts. Gift giving isn't just about the gift itself; it is what the gift signifies. For those of us who are gift givers, giving and receiving the perfect gift or gesture shows that we are known, cared for, and prized. The act of sacrifice and investment behind thoughtful gift giving is sacred, but a thoughtless gift, a missed birthday or anniversary, or a lack of reciprocation can be disastrous for relationships involving gift givers. That's why Christine feels isolated and alone, unappreciated and unloved. The problem for Christine is that even if her guests tried to thank her or reciprocate, nobody could live up to her own standards.

Think of it this way. When you are the one throwing the party, you are in control and you set the standard. This is true for any of us, regardless if we are extroverts or introverts. And those standards can be hard to live up to. In a sense, Christine has lavished such attention on her friends that they would be hard put to reciprocate. In another sense, Christine was suffering from that "lonely in a crowd" feeling many of us can fall into from time to time.

> Christine was suffering from that "lonely in a crowd" feeling many of can us fall into from time to time.

The reality is, Christine is looking for love in all the wrong places. She has defined her worth through relationships measured by gifts, expressions of thoughtfulness, and the frequency of social gatherings. But the question for Christine is, "Who am I without others?" Thoughtfulness and care expressed through gifts are the currency through which she has found worth and belonging . . . but what if there was another way?

JOY, CELEBRATION, AND GIVING

Perhaps your love language is, in part, expressed through gifts. If that is the case, there likely is a part of Christine's vicious cycle that rings true for you. God wants you to know that you have worth and that you belong—that is God's great gift to you. You "belong" to God as a gift. You don't have to work to impress God, you don't have to have the apartment decorated or the right play mix streaming for God to come into your heart. God has wanted to belong to you and you to Him since the beginning. Part of the reason there is a bit of a gift-giver in all of us is because we have been created in the image of a gift-giving God. It's in His nature and essence to love—there can be no real experience of love without giving.

This is what is so exciting about a relationship with God: we get to constantly give and receive! A relationship with God is not primarily about rules and expectations, rituals and religious jargon. It is about joy and celebration expressed through receiving and giving. Remember, the God who created it all is intimately engaged with you and demonstrates this through love, even when we are not perfect, when we are, by others' standards, unlovable because of the things we've done. Or not done. Or not been.

> There is a bit of gift-giver in all of us because we have been created in the image of a gift-giving God.

One of the most famous stories Jesus ever told is the story of a son who breaks his father's heart to the core. After a life of giving his son love, honor, respect, and all the earthly security money can buy, the son packs up everything and moves out to live a life of pleasure and partying. He turns his back on his father, the family business, his brother, and all the great traditions and heritage he had. He longed to live a different kind of life, to experience the party culture of a foreign people, and he gets his wish. Cashing in everything he had, he wastes his time and money in drunkenness and sex parties, which quickly eats through his life savings. In the end, he finds himself experiencing foreign culture— okay, starving—as a farmhand feeding pigs. While he has no interest in a relationship with his father, he begins to reason that the farmhands who worked for him at his own family farm at least had enough to eat. He plans to go back to his father as a day laborer and makes the long trek back to the family farm. That's where we pick up the story:

> But while he was still a long way off, his father
> saw him and was filled with compassion for him;

48

he ran to his son, threw his arms around him and kissed him.

The son said to him, "Father, I have sinned against heaven and against you. I am no longer worthy to be called your son."

But the father said to his servants, "Quick! Bring the best robe and put it on him. Put a ring on his finger and sandals on his feet. Bring the fattened calf and kill it. Let's have a feast and celebrate. For this son of mine was dead and is alive again; he was lost and is found." So they began to celebrate.[1]

WHEN WE ARE AT OUR WORST

The son, in the midst of his realization, uses a religious word that has lost a lot of its meaning in today's culture—sin. He says that he has "sinned against heaven" and against his father. This son has done lots of things wrong—he broke his father's heart, wasted his inheritance, turned his back on his brother and family business, and brought shame to their name by becoming famous at partying. Sin, however, goes deeper than just the way he caused pain. Sin is something within us, a drive deep inside us that gives rise to the things we do. Sin is like a disease, a cancer of our soul, and even though some people are good at hiding that cancer, eventually it shows. It pops up as an outburst of anger, daydreaming about harming others, or using others for our own pleasure. It pops up as we take what isn't ours, lie to others around us, and tear them up with our gossip and cruel posts online. These actions are the effects of sin, the symptoms of the cancer eating us up from the inside out.

The disease of sin has its symptoms . . . but so does love.

Love is also something deep within us, a yearning for beauty and for everything to be made right. And through God's deep love and forgiveness, we can be set free from sin's grip. That's what we see here in this story.

Because of the father's love for the son, as soon as he sees him, filled with compassion, he leaps into action. The father thinks of his son's return as a second chance, as if his son who was as good as dead has come back to life! The father's response? A party with extremely special and symbolic gifts. The gifts the father gives the son are not just material possessions—they represent relationship. The ring was a special ring representing the family's power over financial and contractual transactions. The robe would have differentiated the son from the day laborers and employees; it would have shown others that he was an insider, a member of the family. The fattened calf was a special animal reserved typically for holidays when family and friends would have gathered. The father expresses his love in the form of celebration, joy, and special, meaningful gifts. "Let's have a feast and celebrate!" These are the words of a gift giver who is overflowing with joy—and this is *exactly* how God looks at the possibility of a relationship with you.

GETTING WHAT WE DON'T DESERVE

What makes this story so incredible is that the son did not deserve the things he received. If anything, the son should have gotten the opposite. If we were writing the story, we would have made the son suffer, at least for a short time, to teach him a lesson. Make him sleep in the barn. If we were writing the story, we would have made him pay back what he squandered. Or maybe we would have refused to take him in. The story turns common sense on its head because it springs out of another idea we've lost track of in modern-day society—grace. Grace in the Bible is seen through expressions of love from God. These expressions of love from God to us have nothing to do with whether or not we are worthy of them. In fact, normally grace is given in the shadow of our unworthiness. These gifts are given to us not on the basis of anything we've done but simply because God desires to give them. Grace. Grace tells us that we have worth and that we belong. Grace. Grace is confusing because the world and

> We believe we belong only when we have something to contribute . . . but that's not how God's love works.

every fiber of our flesh tells us that our worth is tied to what we bring to the party. We believe we belong only when we have something to contribute . . . but that's not how God's love works. God loves you. God expresses that love through the gift of grace. He says let's have a feast and celebrate.

REFOCUS:
Coming back to God

Christine may have had to work to maintain the appreciation of her friends. You may feel the same pressure. But that is not how a relationship with God works. God is the one who invites us to relationship, to feasting and celebration. God has created us to both give *and* receive—a relationship with God stirs joy in us through the very exchange we experience in a love relationship with Him. We become lovers in the process of giving and receiving, releasing and embracing. This is where joy lives, in the exchange!

Joy and celebration are at the absolute center of God's plan for you and the world. How do we begin a relationship with God? We *come back.* The son "came to his senses" and came back to his father. We do this when we realize that only God can give us what we so desperately need—love. Love comes to us as a gift of grace from God. God loves us. He tells us we have worth, that we belong at His table. The Bible is filled with many illustrations of this, but none more familiar than that single, simple verse made famous in football stadiums across America, John 3:16–17, which says, "For God so loved the world that he gave his one and only Son, that whoever believes in him shall not perish but have eternal life. For God did not send his Son into the world to condemn the world, but to save the world through him." Again, try placing your name into these verses and re-read God's gift of grace to you. God loves the world and He loves you.

God's love, John 3 tells us, is expressed through the gift of God's Son, Jesus. Jesus is God's greatest gift to us because Jesus saves us from the punishment of perishing and gives us eternal life. Jesus can show us a better way of living. Through Jesus, we can be included in the family of God, dressed in the beauty of the family robe. Through Jesus, our souls can feast on the only thing that can truly satisfy us—love.

TAKING THE FIRST STEP

You can come back to God by believing that God is good, that He loves you, and that you *need* Him. God gives Jesus to us to make this possible. When God gave Jesus to the world, He gave Him knowing that He would be murdered in our place, nailed to a cross, and carried off to the graveyard. Yet He still gave Jesus. Jesus died our death to pay the penalty for our lack of love, for turning our back on God, and for all the evil we've done to others and to ourselves. God simply loves back, even when we are at our worst.

Just as important, however: After Jesus was murdered, He returned to life. That is what Easter is all about. It's why we feast and celebrate every year at Eastertime because Jesus came out of the graveyard, completely conquering death. This is the most basic and important message of the Bible, something we call "the gospel," which means good news. We can experience God's grace by embracing this simple truth. We can start again, as it were, by "coming to our senses" and returning to our Heavenly Father who longs to dress us and feed us with Jesus. Practically, we do this when we . . . *ask*. The son who returned to his earthly father experienced radical and unexpected love expressed through mercy and grace. This is why he said these words, likely in tears, "Father, I have sinned against heaven and against you.

I am no longer worthy to be called your son." He recognizes his wrong, which allows him to receive the grace and mercy of his father's love.

INTO A LIFE OF LOVE

You can do this too. God is waiting to receive you and shower you with the greatest gift He can possibly give— new life through His Son, Jesus! Don't you want to come back into the party, to truly belong and find your worth through a relationship of love? If so, consider saying these words out loud to your Heavenly Father. He sees you, He loves you, and He longs to receive you back.

> "Father, I have walked away from You—forgive me. I have done things I shouldn't have done and not done the things I knew in my heart I should have done. I want to come back and receive Your great gift of Jesus. I believe Jesus died my death. I believe He was raised from the graveyard. Come into my life and lead me. Help me to follow you into a life of love. Amen."

CHAPTER 4

You Belong: Embraced for God

LOVE LANGUAGE: PHYSICAL TOUCH

WHEN WAS THE LAST TIME YOU WERE touched in a positive way?

Touch is a powerful thing. We know that tactile inter-action with infants is essential in brain development, and without being embraced, babies will likely develop all sorts of mental and emotional disorders and deficiencies. The need for touch is hardwired into our souls and without it, over time, we devolve into something less than human.

Today, real, concrete human touch can feel like a special treat in this era of virtual connection. And yet . . . touch is tricky. We live in a world where we both crave for and cringe at physical touch. What may seem like a friendly hug or

> We live in a world where we both crave for and cringe at physical touch.

pat is really a sexual pass or, even worse, a form of abuse. What is meant as a form of welcome can be misconstrued as a violation. Physical touch is riskier than it's ever been to both give and to receive, yet we were made for it, we crave it. Just ask Lance.

Lance is a homeless, alcoholic Army vet who lives in a park with all his earthly possessions packed into a shopping cart. Lance doesn't remember the last time he was truly touched in a positive way, let alone the last time he was physically embraced. Hugged. Wrapped in the arms of another.

Embrace is a form of touch that melts our hearts and lets us know that we truly belong to someone. There is likely no better picture of what embrace means than when a child embraces her father. We picture her in a full-on run, latching onto him with both arms with a look of joy and trust as she hugs tight.

It had been so long for Lance, however, that he had forgotten all about the experience. In a stupor, Lance fills his days in the park begging money from the families and lovers strolling hand in hand. It is no surprise that the money he often receives is a sort of payoff to keep from interacting with him. People drop money into his hands with their eyes down. Many walk across the park opposite of Lance to avoid paying this toll. Lance and all the Lances of our world are the unembraceables, the untouchables of our time. They have forgotten what it is like to be embraced, to truly belong to another. As obvious as this is for homeless people, the reality is we are surrounded by millions of people who are suffering a drought of physical touch.

Single people, for instance, are often not embraced for good. For many singles, settling for inappropriate touch or meaningless sexual encounters does nothing to fill the deep hole in their hearts that can only be filled by transformative embrace. Oftentimes, the elderly long for the physical touch they used to take for granted but has now vanished with the passing of a spouse or the displacement from their immediate family or friends as they transition to end-of-life living arrangements. The reality is, we live in a dry and thirsty land where appropriate and fulfilling physical touch has all but vanished.

THE BEST (AND WORST) OF OUR NEED FOR TOUCH

Touch is so much more than tactile sensation. It is one of the most powerful ways we know we belong to another. All around us are people who can't remember the last time they experienced true embrace. To be embraced, deeply embraced, is to be held tightly, to be held enthusiastically, to be held with deep unspoken meaning. In this experience, we know that we belong; we have a place in the presence of someone. People who speak the love language of physical touch know this all too well. From hugs, pats on the back, holding hands, or thoughtful brushes, they long to give and get love in a physical way! Touch for them shows belonging, concern, and love. For those of us who love through touch, embrace isn't just nice, it is crucial, and without it there is a void that nothing else can fill. Physical touch for all people should foster a sense of security and belonging in our relationships—it is one of the essential ingredients for a life well lived, a life that is full and flourishing.

Physical touch, however, is one of the most frequent ways we harm and are harmed. Whether it is in the form of sexual abuse, molestation, physical abuse, or physical intimidation, touch is far more often associated with harm than being embraced for good. This makes it tricky to think about experiencing love with others and from God through the window of touch. Yet we were made for embrace, we crave it deep in our bones. Whether we've been deeply harmed by inappropriate touch or are rotting from the outside in, like Lance, for lack of embrace, one thing is true—*we need to be embraced for good.*

Being embraced for good restores our souls; it rescues us from isolation, fear, loneliness, and despair. We know this from an early age, the first time we have a bad dream or see the boogeyman in the shadows of our dark bedroom—we cry and long to be sheltered in the embrace of a loving parent. To be embraced for good is essential to our sense of well-being. The great news is that no matter what our experience is with touch, whether we have been harmed or are longing for more, there is a kind of embrace we can experience from God that fills us up and makes us know at the core of our being that we belong.

IN DESPERATE TIMES, GOD SHOWS UP

Throughout history, God has made Himself known in many ways. Some of these ways have been spectacular and other ways quite hidden to the vast majority of people. It seems like when we need it most, God reveals Himself and allows us to "feel" His love. There is a book in the Bible called Jeremiah where God's people found themselves in a desperate place. They were in the midst of a crisis and needed to "feel" God, to know deep down He was with them. They were at the end of a losing war and were just about to be captured and transported to a foreign land to serve the great superpower of their day. While the circumstances of this defeat and captivity were incredibly complex, one thing was sure: the people who were looking to God needed to know they still belonged to Him, and that He would be with them now and in their future captivity.

When the people are at their lowest point, feeling hopeless, they remember this: "The LORD appeared to us in the past, saying: 'I have loved you with an everlasting love; I have drawn you with unfailing kindness.'"[1] God reminds them that He has always loved them in a special way, an everlasting way. Further, He says that He has "drawn" them with unfailing kindness. God has never failed them but has drawn them, which literally means to be led by embrace. They were always led by embrace through a kindness that never failed, and God makes it clear during this time of crisis that He would lead them into the future. This is what it means to be embraced for good by God. It is like a hug from Him at the right moment.

EMBRACED FOR GOOD

In your life right now, you are being "hugged" by God whether you know it or not. God is hugging you, holding you tight, embracing you for good and leading you with His never-failing kindness. We may not always be looking for this hug, but we are getting it. God has come running, falling on us enthusiastically and showering us with kindness and love. To be embraced for good by God is transformative and we can feel it deep down in our bones.

> In your life right now, you are being "hugged" by God whether you know it or not.

I'll never forget when I (York) woke up with an ache in my bones from another night of sleeping in a cold van during a season of home- lessness. We had been living in a park, eating nothing more than cereal for days in mid-October. We were desperate. And while we weren't looking for a hug from God, I person- ally was desperate for any kind of hope that the day would be different than the ones before. With a thick frost on the windshield of the car, strong rays of light began to penetrate the trees and melt the frost. Soon, a beautiful mist rose from the frost as beams of light invaded the darkness and damp cold of the van. In this one moment as a child, all the cer- tainty I had from my parents about atheism was challenged. It was as if I was receiving a literal hug from God, or at least the universe.

Looking back, I believe that moment was a time when the very presence of God was invading my life circumstances and I was being wrapped in the warm hug of a God who loved me and wanted to change my circumstances. At times, all of us need that hug from God, particularly during times of loneliness, despair, loss and grief, and fear.

Back to Jeremiah's story of the people facing desperate times. God continues to say this to those going through this time of crisis:

> "See, I will bring them from the land of the north
>   and gather them from the ends of the earth.
> Among them will be the blind and the lame
>   expectant mothers and women in labor;
>   a great throng will return.
> They will come with weeping;
>   they will pray as I bring them back.
> I will lead them beside streams of water
>   on a level path where they will not stumble."[2]

As they lose the war and are carried to a land that seems like it is on the other side of the earth, God promises to lead the people by embrace, particularly those who need it most. The blind, the lame, the uber-pregnant moms—a great throng of hurting and helpless people! These are the kinds of people God gives special attention to: those who need a hug the most. They will cry tears of joy, praying as God restores them to a place of safety, beside streams of water on level paths where they will not stumble.

Do you feel like you need a hug from God? Do you feel like one of the blind, lame, and vulnerable Jeremiah talks about here? Good news: God's love is kind, it doesn't fail, and He is hugging you, even right now.

REFOCUS:
You have a place in God's heart

So, what do we do when we get a hug from God? HUG BACK! That's what the people in Jeremiah's day did—they "returned" with weeping and prayer. We hug back when we respond to God's presence. God has placed the need for physical touch deep down within us because this is how He wants to be loved as well. We can touch God and be touched by Him as we are embraced and embrace back. We do this through what we call "worship." More powerful than being held with physical arms, the embrace of God is felt deeply when we worship Him. Worship is the number one way we can experience physical touch from an invisible God! That is how the people in Jeremiah's story responded back to God: "This is what the LORD says: 'Sing with joy for Jacob; shout for the foremost of the nations. Make your praises heard, and say, "LORD, save your people, the remnant of Israel.""[3] God's people hug back through worship.

God wants you to know, at the core of who you are, that you belong to Him. You have a place in His world and in His heart! He also wants you to respond back to Him. Have you ever given a hug and in the midst of that embrace felt like you were giving but not getting back? That the other person was not really responding? Most of us have. Now, we can never out-hug God, but we can respond appropriately. God's people hug back through worship. Worship is more than singing and praying, but it certainly includes those things. We worship God through our work, our attitudes, how we treat others, how we spend our time and money—everything in our lives can and should be an act of worship.

Having said this, worship in its simplest form is simply us hugging God back. The love language of physical touch certainly includes human-to-human, tactile touch, but there is a deeper, more fulfilling way we can have our tank filled. We can be transformed through embrace through deep, meaningful worship. We can physically hug God back by getting our bodies involved in this worship. We can use the words of our mouths to physically tell God that we love Him too. We can sing to Him as well. We can clap our hands, jump up and down, and even yell a little bit—or a lot! Getting our bodies involved in responding to God allows us to "feel" God's hug, an embrace that is truly transformative. As we "feel" God through worship, we get a deep, convincing sense that we truly belong to Him.

THE TOUCH WE WERE MADE FOR

Through experiencing the embrace of God, we can move from a sense of isolation and uncertainty to knowing that we belong. We can go through times of deep crisis with a sense of God's presence, knowing that, no matter what, God will continue to lead us with an unfailing kindness. Physical touch is at the center of human relationships, but it is also how we can experience the embrace of God. We can be embraced for good as we respond to God's work in our lives. Singing and praying are just two examples of how we can involve our bodies in a relationship with God. Some people, as they run or work out, do so as a response to God. Artists, as they paint or dance, do so as an expression of passion back to God. Medical practitioners, postal workers, law enforcement professionals, and ride-sharing drivers can do their physical activities throughout the day as expressions of worship to God too. Whether we are wielding a stethoscope, throwing packages on people's porches, handling difficult and dangerous circumstances, or driving someone to the airport, all physical activity can be "devoted" to God, expressions of worship.

When we devote our physical selves to God, we literally hug God back, and in this embrace, we experience Him in a powerful way. In its simplest and often easiest expression, however, we can hug God back by acknowledging His presence through prayer and song. Singing and praying are a core part of a relationship with God. These practices allow us to feel God drawing us to Himself. This is how God touches us and we touch Him in a way that is actually more real than the touch we experience from those around us. This kind of touch never crosses the line, never arouses suspicion or anxiety. This touch never violates trust or causes harm—it is the touch we were made for and often don't realize we need because we've gone without it for so very long.

CHAPTER 5

You Are Known: Experiencing True Togetherness with God

LOVE LANGUAGE: QUALITY TIME

IN 2009, AMERICA WAS HIT WITH A SUDDEN PANIC. This panic was due to an outbreak of a rarely heard of illness called "swine flu." You may or may not remember it, but for many, that season of life was characterized by deep concern, isolation, and unusual precautions. Suddenly, in movie theaters, restaurants, airports, and shopping malls, waterless soap dispensers sprang up. Signs in each and every bathroom in America urged the public to wash hands vigorously. The lucky few who could get a swine flu vaccine rushed to do so, while many others chose to forgo the fashion faux pas and discomfort and wore medical masks in public. It was a season of panic and precaution, but thankfully, this epidemic quickly vanished, as did our memory of it.

Just like with the swine flu, every now and then a new virus strain emerges that makes the news and spurs fears of an outright epidemic spreading. Most recently we were faced with the COVID-19 global pandemic, something that will likely have an impact on us for generations. The modest precautions we took during the "swine flu" were modified and multiplied exponentially in the COVID-19 outbreak. However, there is another global malady that is also life-threatening. It comes with no warnings from the Centers for Disease Control. We can't take a pill or shot to immunize ourselves from it, and no amount of isolating ourselves from those who already have it will prevent us from catching it—in fact, isolation may be the worst thing we could do for this contagion.

In short, we are witnessing an outbreak of loneliness. It may not feel as drastic as "sheltering in place" during a medical emergency, but its effects were certainly noticed and multiplied by the deadly events that shaped our world in 2020. Loneliness in our time has reached an epidemic level, and the impact is real and severe.

According to the best medical research, loneliness has real and serious consequences: "Humans are naturally social. Yet, the modern way of life in industrialized countries is greatly reducing the quantity and quality of social relationships," and further, "Social relationships, or the relative lack thereof, constitute a major risk factor for health—rivaling the effect of well-established health risk factors such as cigarette smoking, blood pressure, blood lipids, obesity and physical activity."[1] Furthermore, the impact of loneliness itself leads to other problems. "Lonely adults consume more alcohol and get less exercise than those who are not lonely. Their diet is higher in fat, their sleep is less efficient, and they report more daytime fatigue. Loneliness also disrupts the regulation of cellular processes deep within the body, predisposing us to premature aging."[2] This pandemic has hit hard and fast, with 3 of 4 Americans reporting struggling with loneliness and the associated problems that come with it.[3] The problem is so widespread in the United Kingdom that in 2018 they appointed their first national Minister of Loneliness, Tracy Crouch.

BUSY, POPULAR, LONELY

Tyler is a great example of the pandemic of our time. To know Tyler, one would never think he could possibly be one of the lonely. Tyler is popular, surrounded by people both online and in his day-to-day activities. Just a few years out of college, Tyler spends nearly all of his nonworking hours with a host of people who share mutual interests. Tinkering with computer software, online video games, and thrift store hunting, Tyler rarely runs out of things to do. Why is he such a great illustration of the lonely in our time? For Tyler, time spent with others never seems to fill his tank— it is never enough, and deep down he longs for something more, though he can't quite place his finger on it. Tyler has begun to realize that no matter how much time he spends and with whom he spends his time, there is always a deep hole of loneliness at the end of each day. Tyler is longing for something more than what he can find in his relationships, even his best relationships.

For good reason, Tyler's dilemma is not foreign to us. Most of us can relate to feeling lonely while being surrounded by people. Like water pouring over sand, our time spent with others frequently runs right through our souls, leaving us just as dry and dusty afterwards as we were before.

The reality behind loneliness for people like Tyler and the rest of us is that we were made for something more. We were created to have a quality relationship with God and when that is missing, no number of friendships, even deep friendships, can ever fill the void. Without a relationship with God, our other relationships are like water pouring over sand. We can pour and pour and pour into them, but they never seem to fill up. They never seem to create anything truly meaningful or lasting.

What's more is that our relationships, even our best ones, often betray us. There likely isn't a person among us who can say they've never been deeply hurt, wounded, abandoned, or betrayed by someone they knew, trusted, and even loved. This is not to say we can't have meaningful relationships with other people, but to truly be satisfied, deep in our souls, all other relationships must come second to our first relationship—our relationship with God. This is what we were made for. All other relationships have their best chance at flourishing only when our relationship with God is primary. Our relationship with God is the lens through which we can truly understand and operate within all earthly relationships.

JESUS SAID, "YOU'VE GOT TO PUT ME FIRST"

Jesus said, "If anyone comes to me and does not hate father and mother, wife and children, brothers and sisters—yes, even their own life—such a person cannot be my disciple."[4] Yes, He really said that. He said this while He was surrounded by lots of new people. He had just left a very exciting party and there were suddenly all sorts of people tagging along for all sorts of reasons. Do you think Jesus *really* meant that they should actually hate their loving parents? Do you think

Jesus *really* means that we should hate our siblings? No. Jesus often used an intentionally abrasive, in-your-face style of communicating to get people's attention and jar them out of assumed patterns of thought—particularly when it came to our relationship with God!

Often, we become so used to a way of thinking and feeling that the only way to consider a different perspective is to get a wake-up call—and that is what Jesus' words are: an intentional wake-up call about the importance of putting God first.

What Jesus means here is that if our relationship with Him isn't primary, doesn't make all other relationships pale in comparison, we can't really know Him or follow Him. Jesus is not being selfish or unrealistic, He is stating a matter of fact. Our relationship with Him must be unique. It has to be special in a way that makes even our most treasured relationships, like our family ties, seem hostile by comparison.

Jesus also uses the word "disciple." In our day, this word has only religious meaning, but in Jesus' day, the word was used to describe anyone who was radically following someone else for any sort of profession. You could be a "disciple" of a mason, a jeweler, a carpenter . . . it is simply a term to reflect a level of devotion that is intense, prolonged, unique, and singular. One could never be a disciple of both a mason *and* a jeweler.

To be a disciple required putting everything else second, being laser-focused on following the example and instruction of your employer for a prolonged period of time. We think of this singular, intense kind of commitment required of medical interns in residency and it makes sense to us—that level of devotion is vital if they are to truly learn and immerse themselves in their life-enhancing, life-saving profession. You can't devote your time to multiple professions and expect to become an expert simultaneously in all of them. You can't devote your relational time to God and others equally and expect to be the person God created you to be.

THE CURE FOR LONELINESS

We've been uniquely designed to have a first love, a relationship that is unique with God, and to become experts at mimicking Him, particularly mimicking Him in the way He loves. This is what Jesus is really talking about. Jesus actually wants us to love our parents and siblings and even people we'd consider enemies. Jesus never wanted us to hate one another, but by comparison, the love we have for others needs to pale radically compared to the all-consuming love and devotion we express toward Him.

But here's the secret: When our relationship with God comes first, all earthly relationships suddenly make sense and take their proper place in life. This is where the love language of quality time enters in. Quality time requires giving that special someone your undivided attention—reassuring them by the way you spend time with them and the amount of time you spend with them.

Quality time sparks something magical—a sense of *togetherness*. Togetherness is the immunization from the disease of loneliness. Togetherness is transformative, reversing the isolation of our souls and even reversing the impact of the disease in our cells because it comes with communion with God and companionship with others. "Togetherness" is a powerful idea, but it flies in the face of what most people tend to think of when they think of relationships. As we give God our undivided attention, as we treasure Him, we deepen our relationship with Him and experience this sense of togetherness.

Finally, in this experience we are filled to the brim, even overflowing. Unlike water pouring over sand, when we experience togetherness with God we find a clarity and joy we could never have imagined before. We've been created for this and we hunger and thirst for it, even when we don't know that this is what we are longing for!

Many people don't want to pay the price to experience this togetherness. They can't bring themselves to be singularly devoted to Jesus. The people who started tagging along with Jesus after the party are a good example. They were not "disciples"; they had no intention of being devoted to Jesus and were unwilling to pay the price of discipleship to experience togetherness with Him. They simply had a good time at a party with Jesus and thought it would be exciting to tag along. As they tagged along, Jesus wanted them to know He was not interested in fans. Jesus is not interested in the hype of knowing lots of people thinly but rather disciples who would be devoted to Him deeply. Jesus is radically committed to quality time, to experiencing togetherness with us.

REFOCUS:
Knowing and being known

The great news is that you can easily take the first steps to experiencing togetherness with Jesus. God is waiting and hoping for you to take the first steps toward togetherness. Every step toward togetherness with God is met excitedly with a disproportionate return from Him. He longs for intimacy with us, to spend a quality and quantity of time with us that makes us who we were made to be.

Unfortunately, in our day, many religious people are nothing more than fans, thinly interested in Jesus for a variety of reasons. They travel with Him from experience to experience but aren't deeply connected to Him. For them, Jesus comes second—second to family, second to making money, second to ambitious goals. Quality time is the number one way we can see the difference between a fan and a disciple because disciples *seek to be with* Jesus, to have an ongoing *togetherness* with Him. Part of Tyler's problem and the problem we face with our relationships is that they are thin, superficial—there isn't a true sense of togetherness within them. Togetherness—a profound sense of being *with* and *for* each other, of being seen by the other—is what we crave in our relationships, and when we don't get it, no matter how many people we surround ourselves with, we find ourselves lonely.

Deep within you is a strong desire, a drive to know and be known. You were created first to know God and be known by God and then after that, all your other relationships can find their proper place in life. The biggest reason millions—maybe you—are lonely today is that there is no *togetherness* in your life with God. Togetherness, rich, intimate companionship, comes from spending quality time with Him. This may

> Unfortunately, in our day, many religious people are nothing more than fans, thinly interested in Jesus.

sound like a foreign idea, but spending time with God is literally the number one way to live a life that overflows into love, joy, and peace. A person who is living into *togetherness* with God will experience love, a deep companionship and communion with the one person who can fill them up, even causing them to overflow!

STEP INTO TOGETHERNESS WITH GOD

You can take the first step to experiencing togetherness with Jesus right now. As you've been reading, He has been waiting. Consider doing something real and practical with Him. When we think of quality time with others, often we think of connecting through an activity, a heart-to-heart conversation, or common experience. Perhaps you are in or can get into a physical space where you can do something to connect with God in a tangible way, alone in silence. Start by breathing deeply and slowly. Allow the distractions around you to fade into the background, and simply ask God for His presence. You can say something like, "Jesus, make me aware of Your presence."

As you sit in silence, consider this prayer. Read it slowly and stop.

Your love, LORD, reaches to the heavens,
>   your faithfulness to the skies.
Your righteousness is like the highest mountains,
>   your justice like the great deep.
>   You, LORD, preserve both people and animals.
How priceless is your unfailing love, O God!
>   People take refuge in the shadow of your
>   wings.
They feast on the abundance of your house;
>   you give them drink from your river of
>   delights.
For with you is the fountain of life;
>   in your light we see light.[5]

Read this prayer a second time now and pause. Finally, read it a third time, paying attention to the parts of this prayer that seem to fill you up. When you *feel* specific words in this prayer connecting with your soul, consider them, ponder them, press into them. Ask God why, why these words? What is it about that aspect of this prayer that is connecting with you? As you take this simple step of prayer and meditation on God's Word, you will begin to experience togetherness with Him.

Finally, after you've prayed and meditated on this prayer, consider writing down what you experienced. This act of prayer, meditation, and journaling, writing down, can become an everyday thing, and as you experience togetherness through this simple practice, you will find a longing for it. This practice will fill you up. You will discover it is unlike other relationships, unlike water pouring over sand. Consider doing this daily through the book of Psalms for the next thirty days and watch how you experience the presence of Jesus in your everyday life!

CHAPTER 6

Living into Love

HAVE YOU EVER HAD AN AWFUL, RESTLESS night of sleep? Perhaps you've had the experience of waking up in the middle of the night all alone. You stare up at the ceiling with the glow of your cellphone or alarm clock casting shadows around the room. You toss and turn, hoping to fall back asleep, but your mind gets going. In these moments of restlessness, we come face to face with our humanity. Many of us in these moments feel all alone. In that glow in the middle of the night, our minds swirl around the things we become experts at avoiding thinking about in the busyness of the day. We lie there, wondering about the future, about finances, about health; we worry about relationships, career paths, and retirement. We watch the clock as ten minutes becomes three hours. We watch the ceiling fan spiral above us, we watch the shadows, and in these moments of watching, we wonder and worry about so many things. We've all been there.

Love breaks through our restless watching, our wonder and our worry. Love settles our hearts in a way that mere money can never do. What we need more than a solution, or assurances about the future, is to find hope and peace in *feeling* loved. In the dark moments of our lives, God wants us to know that He is there, loving us and caring for us. Jesus comforted His worrying friends with these words:

> "Therefore I tell you, do not worry about your life, what you will eat or drink; or about your body, what you will wear. Is not life more than food, and the body more than clothes? Look at the birds of the air; they do not sow or reap or store away in barns, and yet your heavenly Father feeds them. Are you not much more valuable than they? Can any one of you by worrying add a single hour to your life?"[1]

WORRY AND WORTH

We can't feel the love of God in our lives unless we realize our value. Jesus doesn't merely say, "Don't worry." He says you have value—you have worth. Worrying is a sign that we believe there is nobody looking out for us, nobody who is caring for us. Deep at the root of worry is the belief that we are invisible, that we don't matter, that we don't have worth. At the root of worry is the belief that we don't belong and that nobody really knows us. None of these things are true. Jesus says that God cares for the birds of the air by meeting all their needs, and if that is how God cares for them, God is caring for you since you are much more important than some random birds!

God loves you deeply. You are seen, you are known, you are loved! As you've read through each of these love language chapters, you probably found yourself connecting at some level with each and every one of them. While we have a dominant love language, love is

> Worrying is a sign that we believe there is nobody looking out for us.

love. Who doesn't feel some sense of worth when we receive a gift? Who doesn't feel seen when someone gives us a kind and affirming word of encouragement? Don't we all feel like we matter when someone does something to help us out or serve us? Regardless of your love language, we *feel* loved when we are *being* loved . . . but the key is to realize it. That is Jesus' point here. When we realize our value to God, we can stop worrying, and as we stop tossing and turning, staring at the shadows of life, we find it possible to *feel* God's love!

SETTING OUR HEARTS TOWARD GOD

God is expressing His love for us all the time—even when we are not aware of it. God is speaking our love language and we can *know or feel* His love as we become aware of His presence in our everyday lives. We can become aware of our value to Him and of His activity in our lives as we seek Him. As we set our hearts and souls toward Him, we can actually experience the wonderful presence of His love. The first step in experiencing God's love is simply to acknowledge that we want to experience His love. This sounds simple but so often, it is the one step people miss. Try saying these words out loud to God right now:

> "Jesus, I want to experience Your love. I believe You died on the cross to pay the penalty for everything I've done and left undone. I believe You conquered death by rising from the grave. I want to know You. Come into my life and lead me in the way of love."

This simple prayer expresses to God our desire to be loved. This prayer recognizes that it is through what Jesus has done for us through His death and resurrection that we can live in love with Him. This prayer acknowledges that we want to live God's way, to be led by Him. This is an important prayer because it opens the door for us to be loved by God. Again, consider saying this prayer out loud to God right now.

God is always loving us, but this prayer tells God we actually want to know His love. Experiencing God's love answers so many of our heart's deepest longings. As we begin to live into love, we find ourselves free from the worries of life. We come to believe that we have worth, that we are seen, that we matter, that we are known, and that we belong! God is speaking our love language and as we receive it, we find hope and peace through Him!

What about the Bible? You may not be a Bible reader yet, but once you open the door of your heart to God's love, you will find that the Bible takes on a whole new meaning. The Bible for most people is just an old book full of genealogies and strange sayings, but when we open our hearts to God's love, the words of the Bible come alive! As you put this book down, consider picking up the Bible and looking for how God is speaking your love language there. Try starting with the book of Psalms and the book of John. Try reading a chapter from each of those two books a day for the next few weeks. Watch for the ways God is reaching out to you, encouraging you, wrapping you in an embrace more powerful than human hands. Look for the ways God is leading you to become a loving person of peace and joy.

Everything changes when we know we are seen, known, and loved. When we feel God's love, we find ourselves transformed from the inside out, and this propels us to join God in what He is doing around us.

What I (York) didn't realize as a child was that every time we burned a Bible on the side of our home, every time we mocked God, every time we turned a blind eye to God's love in our lives, we were literally burning hope, mocking peace, and closing our eyes to the joy and purpose that comes from a life of love. When we experience God's love, we don't merely get warm fuzzies. Feeling God's love isn't about just making ourselves feel better, it is about finding hope, peace, joy, and purpose. When we experience God's love, it does something to us. It electrifies us!

A FIRE IN THE HEART

Some people use the expression "on fire for God." That's what happens when we encounter the love of God: we are "set on fire" in that we get a new source of energy that burns within us! When I (York) finally decided to receive God's love and follow Jesus, immediately I had an unexplainable energy, a fire in my heart. As I read the Bible, prayed, and followed Jesus, I found myself brimming with purpose and hope, and that drove me to love the people all around me. I found myself loving the homeless on our block, loving the prostitute at the bus stop, loving my angry neighbor, my rivals on campus. I began to love my family more deeply and my friends more purposefully. This love within me grew because I had received it from God! We become lovers when we are loved. We can tell people they have worth when we know that we have worth. We can help people know that they are seen because we've been seen by God! There is a near-unexplainable joy that comes when we've been set free from the worries of being invisible or forgotten, or from a sense of worthlessness. When we know we are seen, known, and loved, it sets a fire within us. That is what happens when we love and are loved; it is a friendship that catches fire and, in turn, sets our world on fire as well!

Notes

Introduction

1. "Religious Landscape Study," Pew Research Center, https://www.pew
forum.org/religious-landscape-study/.

Chapter 1: "You Are Loved": The Words That Change Everything

1. Ann Landers, *Wake Up and Smell the Coffee!: Advice, Wisdom, and Uncommon Good Sense* (New York: Villard, 1996), 34.
2. Isaiah 54:10.
3. John 6:35.
4. Psalm 139.

Chapter 2: You Are Seen: You Matter and So Do Your Actions

1. See Gary A. Haugen, *Good News about Injustice: A Witness of Courage in a Hurting World* (Downers Grove, IL: InterVarsity Press, 2009), 25–31.
2. Proverbs 21:21.
3. Luke 12:27–28.

Chapter 3: You Have Worth: The Gift of Being Accepted

1. Luke 15:20a–24.

Chapter 4: You Belong: Embraced for God

1. Jeremiah 31:3.
2. Jeremiah 31:8–9a.
3. Jeremiah 31:7.

Chapter 5: You Are Known: Experiencing True Togetherness with God

1. Julianne Holt-Lunstad, Timothy B. Smith, and Bradley Layton, "Social Relationships and Mortality Risk: A Meta-Analytic Review," *PLoS Med* 7, no. 7 (2010): e1000316, https://doi.org/10.1371/journal.pmed.1000316.

2. John Cacioppo, "Why Loneliness Is Bad for Your Health," interview by Nancy Shute, *U.S. News & World Report*, November 12, 2008, https://health.usnews.com/health-news/family-health/brain-and-behavior/articles/2008/11/12/why-loneliness-is-bad-for-your-health.

3. Dennis Thompson, "3 in 4 Americans Struggle with Loneliness," MedicineNet, December 18, 2018, https://www.medicinenet.com/script/main/art.asp?articlekey=217418.

4. Luke 14:26.

5. Psalm 36:5–9.

Chapter 6: Living into Love

1. Matthew 6:25–27.

About
the Authors

GARY CHAPMAN is the *New York Times* bestselling author of The 5 Love Languages® series. As a counselor and popular speaker, he has a passion for helping people form lasting relationships. He is director of Marriage and Family Life Consultants and his radio program airs on more than four hundred stations. Gary and his wife, Karolyn, live in North Carolina. For more information go to 5lovelanguages.com.

R. YORK MOORE is an artistically gifted speaker, a revivalist, and abolitionist. He serves as Executive Director/Catalytic Partnerships and as National Evangelist for InterVarsity Christian Fellowship. He is the author of several books, including *Do Something Beautiful: The Story of Everything and a Guide to Finding Your Place in It* (Moody Publishers). York became a Christian—leaving atheism—while studying philosophy at the University of Michigan. He has an MA in Global Leadership from Fuller Theological Seminary. He lives in Michigan with his wife and three children. For more information about R. York Moore, visit tellthestory.net and follow him on social media channels @yorkmoore.

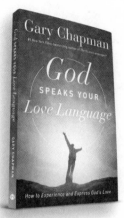